POETRY now

MOMENTS TO SHARE

Edited by

Heather Killingray

First published in Great Britain in 2000 by
POETRY NOW
Remus House,
Coltsfoot Drive,
Woodston,
Peterborough, PE2 9JX
Telephone (01733) 898101
Fax (01733) 313524

HB ISBN 0 75430 917 7
SB ISBN 0 75430 918 5

FOREWORD

Although we are a nation of poets we are accused of not reading poetry, or buying poetry books. After many years of listening to the incessant gripes of poetry publishers, I can only assume that the books they publish, in general, are books that most people do not want to read.

Poetry should not be obscure, introverted, and as cryptic as a crossword puzzle: it is the poet's duty to reach out and embrace the world.

The world owes the poet nothing and we should not be expected to dig and delve into a rambling discourse searching for some inner meaning.

The reason we write poetry (and almost all of us do) is because we want to communicate: an ideal; an idea; or a specific feeling. Poetry is as essential in communication, as a letter; a radio; a telephone, and the main criterion for selecting the poems in this anthology is very simple: they communicate.

CONTENTS

PARADISE

A special place far far away,
Where the sea is clear and the sky is blue,
The red hot sun high above,
Heating the golden brown sand that
Lies on the beautiful shores of the picturesque beach.

Louise Ioannou (13)

THE HARBOUR

Sometimes in life you need some space,
To sit and be alone.
Perhaps you've had a stressful day
Or things were tense at home.

The harbour is my special place,
It's where my dreams can play.
But best of all it stays the same
And calms me as I lay.

I often sit beside the shore
And think of what I choose,
The smell of sea salt fills the air
And blows away my blues.

Then as the night begins to pass
I watch the sun rise high
I feel the warmth upon my face
As daylight fills the sky.

The seagulls gaily swoop and soar
I make myself fly too,
I close my eyes and think sweet thoughts
It isn't hard to do.

Then comes the time to dawdle home
Now calmed and full of glee,
I slowly wander up the lanes
Whilst dreaming of the sea.

Aimee Johnson (16)

CHILDHOOD

Just close your eyes and look around
The wondrous sights of childhood are found.
The green of the grass, the blue of the sky,
The sight of Grandma's home-made pie.
The smiles on children's faces in the park,
The twinkling of stars long after dark.

Just close your ears and look around
The wondrous sounds of childhood are found.
The ice-cream van in the street,
The happy sounds of playing feet.
Children laughing, having fun
The silent sound of the golden sun.

Now sit quite still and breathe in hard,
Smell the washing in your back yard.
Steamed puddings, spotted dick
They smell divine, your lips you lick.
The clean, fresh air all around
The happy memories of smell, sight and sound.

Where have they gone, the days of the past?
Did we realise they wouldn't last?
A quiet moment and they're still quite near
Just close your eyes, you see, they're here.

Lyn Kelly

MY OLD HOUSE

Been over five years, but I can still remember,
Haven't been there since, but in my mind forever?
I remember things I've done, and places I have been,
Things that I have eaten, sights that I have seen.

Moved when I was small, thought I'd be there forever,
I loved playing in the garden, the games I can't remember.
I run in from the garden, Mum's cooking (in my mind's eye)
My sister's fallen over, she's just starting to cry.

Jenny's round, and playing outside, thought we'd be friends forever,
Our cats and dog are alive, and we all are together.
I smell Mum's cooking, making cakes again.
I fall asleep happy, to the sound of rain.

My sister and I argue - drive Mum to the end of her tether,
Our cats aren't dead, we thought they'd live forever.
Over five years later, things have changed, I see.
The only thing left is the memory.

Elizabeth Harling

THE WHITBY ARCADE

The Whitby arcade is my favourite place!
Walk through the door -
Bright outrageous lights.
My face lights up like the lights.
I love the sound of the pinging balls
on the pinball machine,
the crunching of the one arm bandit
and the chinking and clattering of money
as the jackpot falls.
Children cheer when they get a strike
and the ball jets off down the alley,
scattering the skittles like scared cats.
In the distance I can see
waves curling and crashing in the cove.
Screeching, squawking seagulls try to grab
people's fish and chips.
I love the smattering of smells
the salty smell of the sea
the sweet sugary smell of doughnuts and candyfloss
the smell of cod and smoked kippers
drifting past my nose.

All the time, I dream of Whitby.

Hannah Barnett (8)

MY SPECIAL PLACE

When I think of my special place only one place comes to mind,
The creamy white walls and the grey decks,
The big brown cupboard,
The dusty floors,
The dark green curtains,
A room full of girls in horrible grey uniforms,
The group of girls screaming and running around,
The strong smell of board pens surrounding the room,
The sound of someone tapping away at the computer,
The look of the girl sitting staring out of the window,
The group in the corner rushing their homework before next class,
The girls singing the latest song or talking about the latest groups,
The teacher pacing the hall checking in on us,
Girls doing each other's hair,
Someone surfing the net,
Another writing I love? On the board,
Then everyone rushes out the door, the room is quiet and still,
Until another day.

Alene Buckle (13)

A CHILD IN THE 60S

I remember when my corner shop was a grocers' store,
with an old-fashioned bell that tinkled when the door opened.
The floor was bare floor-boarding and seemed to be
covered with sacks of all kinds -
potatoes, onions, carrots and the like.
What I remember most about the store was
the ever present aroma of coffee beans.
The street outside was a cobbled road
where the weekly washing would be hung,
there draped drying for everyone to see.
The lamps at the end of the street were gas
and a man came round every evening to light them.
Our house was a two up two down inner terrace
with an outside toilet we shared with other families.
We had no bathroom and it was grand on cold days
to sit in the tin bath in front of the coal fire.
Having the water topped up now and again
with newly boiled water was sheer heaven.
Today we shop in supermarkets,
being served by assistants more resembling robots.
We live in roomy houses,
with all mod cons and central heating.
We have washing machines and tumble dryers.
Unlimited hot and cold water on tap.
But there's no precious smells like the past.
It's not the same kind of living somehow.

Carol Noble

SENSING A SPECIAL PLACE

I know a place where I long to be,
Somewhere down inside me.

I don't know how to get there,
That place that's in me somewhere.

I've been there once but never again;
It seems like heaven, but it's not the end.

I'll get there soon I know I will,
Even if I must climb a hill.

I know a place where I long to be,
Somewhere down inside me.

Kimberly Benham (11)

MY SPECIAL PLACE

My family have a special place,
That is to all our taste.

Each Sunday morn the bell rings out,
And calls us all to join together
To worship our Lord.

I love to look at the stained glass windows,
And admire the new chairs and tiled floors.

The organ plays some lovely hymns,
The choir sings sweet and clear,
For we are worshipping Him.

The vicar gives us all a blessing
For now we have all learnt the lesson.

Hannah Underwood (11)

THE PLACE

Interesting and factful
Things for us to learn
My favourite place in the whole wide world
Is the museum.
Dinosaurs and animals
Wars and things from the past
Then we come to outer space
And look at all the stars.
So by reading this poem
You should see
The museum is the best place to be.

Abby Davis (7)

THE PURR-FECT CAT

Curled up in a ball on top of my bed,
Pokes out a little black, fragile head,
His moonlit eyes contrast his shade,
And his feline physique is worth A in grade,
He is special, cuddly, affectionate and cute,
There was never a cat with a cuddlier suit,
The gift that he left me last night in the hall,
Shows this moggy tries hard to accommodate us all,
But how would you like a gift left in your shoe,
A nice furry mouse or even a shrew?
A dead creature is not a diamond ring,
But he brought it for me and that is the thing,
It is the thought that counts and not what it is,
But next time I'd prefer if he keeps his rodents his!

Philip Joyce

DEAR PARTNER

I am so pleased I've found you, I want you to know
I am never going to let you go

I've fought long and hard to have you by my side
It has not been a particularly easy ride

When I thought I could try nor take no more
One look in your eyes would show me a new door
And I strive to hold you and fight our evil war

The many rugged mountains we struggled to climb
Have been difficult, painful and troublesome times

Your smiling face just makes me melt, this is how I've always truly felt
Tarot cards educated me that you to me were dealt

When morning dawns and I open my eyes
I'm so grateful to have you lying by my side

The warmth of your skin when it touches mine
Make my whole body glow and my love outwardly shine
Upon your love I dearly love to dine

The gift you give me is within yourself
Nothing could match it in money or wealth

When returning from work your cuddle and kiss
Is something I long for all day as you I dearly miss
That cuddle and kiss leaves me in a moment of sheer bliss

My devotion for you grows stronger each day
In your life for eternity I wish to stay

Equally as powerful as love and life with each other
Is the child inside conceived from our passion dear lover
I know nothing or no one will our love again ever smother

So I thank you my dearest for just being you
I love you no more than you are due

I can't wait till the day I hold our baby in my arms
You'll be a wonder father, of this I've no qualms

Deborah Broughton

MY EDUCATION

The best things in life they say are free
But for my education my parents paid the fees.
They struggled and hustled to provide me this legacy
I pray that their souls find peace in eternity.

You never know what treasure you'll find
Until you learn to use your head and your mind
The blessings you'll find in your past tuition
Will always live with you through life's great mission.

Alafie

I KNOW YOU'RE IN THERE SOMEWHERE

When health and independence we have, but take as *red*,
the thoughts of losing either don't journey through our head.
The best things in our lives are these, I look and see that now,
as mind and soul and spirit too, in ailing body row.
I know you're in there somewhere, the *person* not the *face*,
no longer sharing memories since *life* slowed down your pace.
The RAF, the teacher proud, the craftsman through and through,
are parts of your own history book, which go to make up *you*.
You are in the attic now, in suitcase, box or bag,
behind the nineteen twenties clock, a phonograph and rag.
I sort through *you* with feeling's mixed, as in the loft you're *Dad*,
where memories will make me laugh, but also make me sad.
For back on earth, reality is sometimes hard to bear,
when life has dealt its tarnished card, it all seems so unfair.
You're caught, you're trapped within yourself, frustration running high,
no answers to the questions put, no reasons as to why?
I know you're in there somewhere, within your weakening frame,
but what's the point of looking for something or one to blame.
I haven't got a magic wand, to wave, to bring back *you*,
so being there, to show I care, is all that I can do.
When health and independence we have, but take as *red*,
the thoughts of losing either don't journey through our head.
The best things in our lives are these, I stand firm in my view,
and wish for peace within the form . . . the form imprisoning *you*.

Jennifer Ramsey

MY SON

You stand so tall beside me, on the threshold of life.
Memories flicker through my mind, God-given treasures
stored in my heart.

. . . A small head held against my breast, a tiny hand
spread like a starfish.
A puckered face that soon is wreathed in smiles.

. . . A damp, curly head, warm from sleep, two little arms
twined around my neck.
'I love you Mummy,' you often said - worth more to me than all
the money in the bank!

'The next train stop will be at Crewe,' you proudly said.
As you drove Granny thousands of miles - on your *settee special!*

. . . And then to school . . . not always your favourite place!
Homework the bane of your life became, at *Bishop's*
your excuses have brought you fame!

. . . Sand and sea, lots of fun, wonderful holidays with
my dad and mum.
They gave them to you - and their love ever free.

. . . Steam trains, old cars, Star Trek too, Queen and steamboats -
all part of you.
American Football - double Dutch to me, but the pleasure
that it gives you is lovely to see!

. . . You've had your problems - perfect you'll never be.
But I'm so thankful that God entrusted you to me.

Your college days are over, the world is your oyster.
I pray God's blessing upon you, to keep you always in His care.

Just wanted you to know, you are held within my heart.
Dustman or dropout or even millionaire
- I'll always be proud of my son, someone beyond compare.

Margi Hughes

HIDDEN COUNTRYSIDE

Dark, dormant seeds;
Hiding, huddled together
Under the blanket earth.
Watching, waiting,
For change in the weather,
Sleeping silently, significantly slow;
Turning in exact time with the signal to grow.

Creeping out from covers;
Shooting out like fingers;
Stealthily feeling still, chill air around;
Peeping through solid soil cracks without a sound.
Gazing from a loftiness high above,
Tree upon tree commands the scene.
In a stark, gaunt emptiness,
Where the seasons have once been.

In a reflective rhythm
They both combine.
Spring is about to breathe
Beauty into a promise sublime!

Blossoms and buds
Bob onto branches,
Fragrant, young and new;
Pink, white and green in hue.
Sky and earth combine,
Carpets come woven with threads
Of yellow, blue and green
Creating the biggest tapestry
You've ever seen!

Sheila Cundy

SIMPLY THE BEST

It was simply the best day out
When I went to Wembley to see,
The football team that I support
Come away with a victory.

It was simply the best night out
Meeting up with my friends at the fair
Where there were rides, stalls and hot-dogs
In fact, just about everything there.

It was simply the best film
That I have ever seen,
The film was called the Titanic
My eyes were just glued to the screen.

It was simply the best holiday
When I decided to go abroad,
To the Costa Del Sol
Where one could never be bored.

It was simply the best fashion competition
That I have entered,
When the judges awarded me second place
I felt quite complimented.

It was simply the best dance
With people there that I knew,
I was invited to have the first dance of the evening
And I won the raffle too.

Ena Page

AT SEA

There is a place I love to be,
It's on a ship away at sea,
In the tropics feeling free.

Far from land in deepest night,
All alone, no ships in sight,
In tropic warmth it does feel right.

A gentle breeze, a cloudless sky,
The shining stars attract the eye,
While hearing water slipping by.

To see each day sunsets romantic,
And at night's end, dawns dramatic,
Always makes me feel quite ecstatic.

On the sea where fish abound,
Where porpoise leap out all around,
It seems like paradise is found.

During the day, the sun is hot,
I give work and toil not a thought,
But know I am happy with my lot.

R Hogg

CATNAP

We have a senile
friend of a feline,
a ginger she
the cat has had her day,
no more astounds
with leaps and bounds
she just enjoys her siesta.

She was smitten
as a kitten,
with a dust-filled chest
we gave her brandy
from a spoon
EPN'essed
it cured her.
What would Napoleon have said
no matter, he's dead.

The cat purrs on
counting her nine lives,
the shout goes out
to my wife
'Put the cat out!'
'Not on your life, not on your Nelly
it's your turn!'
She rolls on her belly
to watch portable telly.
If one pussy stays in
the other is out of bounds.
I put out the cat, could be on a promise!
The door slams shut behind me
bloody Yale lock.
I feel like Fred Flintstone as it starts to rain,
thinking to myself - *Not tonight Josephine!*

Myk Jonson

IF

If I have a pen, I'll write in the morning,
I'll write in the evening and at twilight;
The lyrics with passionate words.

If I have a pen I'll write in the afternoon,
I'll write in the daytime and at dawn;
The words with lyrics as passionate as you.

If I have a pen, I'll write my lines,
I'll write in the room and in my closet;
The notes with passionate lines to massage your heart.

If I have a pen, I'll write my memoirs,
My memoirs will make your heart beat faster;
Especially when it is congratulating you.

The pen I want must be a golden one,
To write the thrill I got from you.

Dalsie Mullings

HAPPY MEMORIES

Now I've got to 81
I must be kind to everyone.
To smile at neighbours passing by,
Forget my small worries,
I really must try.
For I can sing, and tap my toe,
Although at times
I'm a little bit slow.
A daily walk to the village store
Not too far away.
A coach ride to the seaside,
There and back,
In a day.
See raindrops on the windowpane
Birds splashing in puddles,
Along the lane;
The colourful rainbows
When rainshowers have gone.
In my younger days
No drugs or crime to lead us astray.
Memories come clouding in
I hardly know just where to begin.
The games we played
The friendships we made,
Life changes much, sad we've lost touch,
But my memories are precious to me,
I appreciate all that I have.
New friends I have made,
I have been lucky, along the way,
And give thanks to God for another good day.

Phyl Adams

TWO'S COMPANY, IS THREE A CROWD?

The day Fluffy died I'd said 'That was that
I'd never again get so close to a cat.'

But oh two weeks later and what did I do?
I went to the Cats' Home and came back with two!

Not shiny and smooth as cats ought to be
But skinny and scruffy and with the odd flea.

One was a tabby, and looked very frail,
With very large ears and a great bushy tail.

The other a tortie, so gentle and sweet,
With white on her paws like socks on her feet.

'We are going to be strict!' that's what we had said,
But within half an hour, they were snug on our bed.

I fed them and nurtured them in every way,
But they soon paid us back with such pleasure each day.

The two of them grew to be gorgeous and sleek,
You wouldn't have believed that they'd once been so weak.

I wondered sometimes if they'd pushed things too far,
When their muddy paw prints were left on the car.

Or they'd stay out all hours after a warm sunny day,
And had destroyed my Catnip in their hours of play.

Today ten years later, I have no regrets,
That these lovely creatures became our two pets.

In fact what I'd said was untrue on that day,
Because into our lives has appeared a black stray.

They all saw me coming, the family tell me,
Because instead of no moggies they now number three.

Helen Bott

MOST PRECIOUS OF GIFTS

Would you like a ruby?

No, please can I have a rose?

A sapphire?

no, the sea so blue is the jewel I choose.

An emerald?

The greenest leaves on the trees so tall.

Gold?

let's walk together through the woods,
gold gleams in the Fall.

Silver?

Oh, I love the moon with her silvered beams

A solitaire, a diamond?

but the stars shine full of dreams

A bracelet?

made of buttercup, yellow glowing charm

A castle then, a fortress?

these I find within your arms

Pearls?

those in the cobweb, blushing morning dew

Well, champagne?

that's the water in the cup I share with you

A sequinned dress?

on the grass, raindrops sparkle just like gems

A necklace?

yes, in summertime, of daisy diadems

Some perfume?

oh Norfolk lavender to plant in earth
rich brown

A satin dress?

of silver-birch lace, and fluffy thistledown!

A ring of carat . . .

crescent moon winking with a gleam.

Crystal?

ah, the sunlight, in the glistening stream.

Should I present you with a rainbow?
                              Oh, please my darling do
                              for the rainbow's gem I want to hold -
                              is the baby made with you.

Anita Richards

THE CURRY CLUB

The Curry Club started in College;
The Members of which sought all knowledge -
Of curries and spices;
Seasoning and rices;
And of which Marketplaces to forage.

The Members were ten, they met now and then
To partake or cook - Indian Fare.
Their opinions of food;
Some of them crude;
Were discussed with a knowledgeable air.

The Curry Club held private dinners;
To share curried food with beginners.
The Club grew and grew -
To more than a few,
Turning some into dietary sinners.

There's:-

Tikka Masala; prawn, chicken and lamb;
Soups; Rogan Joshes and Peshwari Naan.
Dansakh; Baltis; Vindaloo;
Tandoori; Chapati; Bhajais too.
Side Salad; Tomato and Vegetable Rice;
Creamed dishes emitting a fragrance so nice
Of lentils and herbs; chilli and pickle;
Relish and chutney; the palate to tickle.

With lots of chatter and old-fashioned natter;
Their stomachs gradually fill.
A leisurely coffee;
A chocolate or toffee;
And a whip round to settle the Bill.

When everyone's dined; lagered and wined;
With contented sighs all round;
The next date and venue
To test a new Menu
Is discussed and proposals abound.

A decision is voted and all diaries noted;
Sadly, the meal meeting ends.
Then, into the night;
All, merry and bright,
Is the parting of Curry Club Friends.

Barbara Paxman

KITTENS TO CATS

I had a litter
of kittens which were bitter.
They were black and white
and always got into fights.

But they soon grew
and the neighbours stopped shouting 'Shoo!'
They are now all really sweet
and still have such tiny feet.

Frances Smith (12)

On Top Of The World

As I stand and stare
The mist around me closes in.
A mist is clammy and oppressive, it clings to you as you move,
But nothing can dim my feeling of satisfaction and ecstasy.
I climbed and strained hour after hour
Over false peaks and rock
Harsh barren, brown rock,
Reflecting the strong rays of the sun.
But after this I feel great
I made it to the top at last
I see the ruins of buildings, a war memorial and hotel.
I stare in wonder,
What was it like to live up here
Or even work up here.
300 feet above this point and the peak would be
Permanently eclipsed with snow.
While I am here I stand in awe
As the whole world is spread out before me,
I can see the rich tapestry of life.
Through the cloud and mist I see the real beauty of the world below.
The view that this huge Fell has witnessed for generations
Taken for granted by some,
To me this is the greatest ecstasy,
I'm on top of the world!

David Hitch

A FINE EXAMPLE

Have you got a moment
To read these lines below?
About a very special person
That I am proud to know.
This person is my father,
He means the world to me,
I trust he knows I'm grateful
For all he's been to me.
He sees some good in everyone
And doesn't criticise,
I've never heard him raise his voice,
Or antagonise
He's always there when needed,
He's time to listen in
And you never have to worry
About his patience wearing thin.
You'd think he had no worries
The way I'm talking here,
But he's had his share of these
Over the passing years.
Mainly ill-health
Of different kinds,
Some being quite frightening
From time to time.
And yet through it all
The worry, the pain
He quietly accepts things
And does not complain.
Should he ever read this
I want him to know

I'll love him forever
That's one thing I know.
Right through the years
He has played his part
And the words I have written
Come straight from my heart.

Janice Sheppard

WATERCOLOURS OF SPRING

Rushing, pushing like a train,
Spring comes surging down the lane,
Rocking, swirling like a storm,
Daisies appear upon the lawn.
Flowing, painting like a brush,
Flying by goes Mother Thrush,
Somersaulting like a clown,
Spills the pretty blossom down,
Swirling, cascading like the stars
Flowers appear in every vase.
On growing, shining apple bowers,
Grow pupils of dilating flowers,
Rushing, pushing like a train,
Spring comes surging down the lane.

Jean Hatton

SEPTEMBER MORN

Have you been to the blackberry patch
on a mid-September morn?
When spiders have set up their webs,
and some are easily torn . . .

You reach to pluck a blackberry fair
when suddenly it's not even there . . .
It's turned to juice . . . right where you stand.
Now, dark blackberry stains cover my hand.

Carol Olson

DOGS

Dogs' loyalty is unbounded
Unquestioning, no retributions.
Loving you - warts and all.
Giving you undivided attention
Watching your movements,
Uncannily sensing habits and moods.
They desire to stay close to you,
Lying on your feet at night,
Absorbing your warmth and being,
Is their idea of paradise.
Dogs will go to any lengths
To gain a pat on the head
Or a word of praise
And reward you with eyes
Filled with devotion, like soft pools.
Your bad temper, or behaviour
Is silently accepted.
No criticism's here.
Strays on the street, if shown kindness,
Will reward you with a wagging tail.
Dogs throughout history have laid down their lives
For their owners
Give me a dog anytime
And you have a friend for life.

Jackie Eccleston

MY MUM AND DAD

The best thing in my life is my mum and dad,
Without them I'll be surely sad,
I'll cry all night, I'll cry all day,
I'll cry so much I'll have to say,
'Mum and dad please don't go
Because I love you so much, so
You look after me, you care forever,
You're my best friends, I don't want to lose you ever.
But I am lucky you're here for life and
I will love you all my life.'

Thawheeda Ahmed Khan (11)

BIRDSONG

Birds come into my garden,
Always cheerful, always moving,
Flitting fast from bush to tree,
They are watching out for me,
Coming close yet staying free -

Bringing their songs into my garden,
Chirps and cheeps, quietly happy;
And often louder from a treetop
They say brighter days are coming soon -
'It's spring, it's spring' the saw tits sing.

Up on a tall treetop the cock thrush
Sings for all to learn of his joy.
Carefully he repeats his phrases,
Fearing we might not capture
His first fine careless rapture.

I did not have to buy them,
Nor trap, nor bribe them -
They just came to cheer me,
Flitting happily around the garden -
Who knows, perhaps they simply
                              loved my flowers?

Linda Young

LITTLE CHILDREN

A small child is God's greatest gift
to all of us.
Funny or solemn, innocent or naughty,
they reflect His Spirit.
Care for them, and we share His joy
in their innocence; their unknowing naughtiness.
Hurt them, and we hurt Him.
Each tiny girl and boy
is a celebration of time,
a mirror image of a perfect creation,
and Eternity.
And to abuse them is the greatest crime
that one can perpetrate
against the soul of the future,
against God's Spirit,
and humanity.

Jenny Proom

YOUNG WAYS

Gone are the days of liquorice wood,
Half a crown at the pictures, and for the Queen we stood,
The Beatles were always on 'Top of the Pops'
With buttoned-up tunics and hair drooped like mops,
Postman's Knock at our parties, thunder and lightning at the doors,
All harmless fun, oh I long for once more.

We had picnics in the park every Sunday we could,
Or a trip on the bus, and for the old we all stood.
Two brothers, three sisters my mom and my dad,
No money, no car, but for life we were glad.

Our houses were terraced, our gardens were small,
But six children and a dog there was room for us all.
We left our doors open, only locked them at night,
You could walk through the streets without getting a fright.

In a two bedroomed house we were a little cramped,
And we made up a fire to keep down the damp.
With four girls in one bedroom, mom and dad in the other,
It didn't leave much room for our little baby brother.

When my mum became pregnant with child number six,
We had to move house or we'd be in a fix,
I still didn't have a bed on my own,
I slept head to toe with my sister, and never alone.

I remember the chimney sweep, and the deliveries of coal,
The rag and bone man and a wash from a bowl.
Our toilet was outside with wringer and all,
And a walk up the street, just to make a phone call.

Even now when I think of my childhood gone by
I remember the bonfire, we all made the Guy.
I'm glad as a child I experienced those days,
They were good, compared to our modern ways.
The only thing I haven't had, and still haven't got
Is a bed to myself , because I'm married with the lot.

F Baker

POOLS OF WATER

P uddles in a street,
 P *o* nds in a park.
A c *o* lourful kingfisher
   Tri *l* ling at a carp.
   Impi *s* h gulls,

   Seas r *o* aring.
 A large *f* ertile lake,

  Teeny de *w* drops in the morning.
 Oh sludgy, *a* lways swampy banks
    Can fill wi *t* h dragonflies.
    Lush sandy b *e* aches
     Help to hide c *r* ocodiles with beady eyes.

Laura Farnall (9)

KNARESBOROUGH BY THE RIVER

The sky so blue, the trees so green
No prettier sight have I seen!
It's summertime in all its glory
At Knaresborough by the river.

Falling leaves upon the ground
As I stand to look around
It's autumn time I'll be bound
At Knaresborough by the river.

Winter comes so bleak and cold
The trees turn from young to old!
I still see the beauty there
At Knaresborough by the river.

Then comes March, spring is here!
Birds singing in voices clear
Making life so full of cheer
At Knaresborough by the river.

Summertime arrives once more
To the place that I adore,
Memories remain forever more
Of Knaresborough by the river.

Rose Grist

MY FAVOURITE PLACE

My garden is the very best place that gives me satisfaction,
It brings joy to my soul and I find a great attraction
Working with the soil and getting plants to flower,
Pruning trees, sowing seeds, then hope we have a shower.

I love to stroll in the garden in the evening, after tea
When the honeysuckle smells so divinely unto me,
Or on a warm summer's day, when Philadephus scents the air;
No man-made perfume to me, can ever so compare.

But it's just as exciting on a mild February day,
Viewing in the garden, the Snowdrops and Crocus on display.
I feed the birds with peanuts, apples and seeds,
Water for washing and drinking, supplies all their needs.

I enjoy hearing the chorus of birds singing in the trees,
Or watching the frogs in the pool, as I weed on my knees.
Butterflies on the Buddleia is another wonderful sight,
Spiders spinning intricate webs, and bees are my delight.

I'm so glad I can find happiness in these simple things:
I don't need gaudy jewellery or expensive rings;
I don't like antique furniture or pictures on the wall,
All I need is a load of muck, to grow my lupins tall!

Patricia Forsberg

FIRST GRANDCHILD

Peeping behind the curtain,
Hiding under the table, eyes twinkling.
Spooning his food into his mouth
Or pushing it away with disgust.
Throwing the colourful ball with delight,
Crying disapproval without tears.
Struggling to get up for a hug after a tumble
Showing off with great glee aware he is being watched.
Smelling divine after a bath,
Tousled hair surrounding his bright little face.
Repeating, repeating the words he hears,
Bringing the books to be seen again, again.
Laughing, laughing as he runs towards Daddy
Arms outstretched,
A bundle of delight,
Our first grandchild.

M P Evison

THOUGHTFUL PAWS

Corrie our Westie has a heart of gold,
she's very sweet and not very old.
Now a brush we give her each day,
they say to keep the fleas away.
Corrie likes to play with a hedgehog,
who then pretends to lie like a log.

From the hedgehog jumps many fleas,
Corrie is good at watching these,
Visitors like this make her itch,
you can see her scratch and then twitch.
When with a hedgehog she wants to play,
We try to keep her right away.

Our dog also likes to play a game,
catching aircraft is her aim.
Out in the garden she will rush by,
if an aeroplane overhead does fly.
Without any doubt this venture will fail,
But she will try again wagging her tail.

Corrie barks loudly when people come
But from cars and lorries she will run.
For dinner she eats chicken and rice
And has fun chasing little woodlice.
She has been taught just how to walk to heel
And to our family she means a great deal.

Sue Duckworth

IT'S MY PLEASURE

The aroma of freshly-ground coffee
The taste of newly-baked bread
The warmth of the sun on my body
The kiss of snowflakes on my head
Scuffing through leaves in the autumn
Casserole hot on the hob
Candlelit aromatic baths
Satisfaction in my job
Long brisk walks in the country
A drink at the pub nearby
Church bells calling us to prayer
A rainbow colouring the sky
Planning a daughter's wedding
The birth of a first grandchild
Kissing the nape of a baby's neck
These things drive me wild
With happiness and thankfulness
Knowing I'm so blessed
But my favourite thing of all
The one that I love best
Is something that after all these years
Comes as no surprise
It's the smile on my darling husband's face
And the look of love in his eyes.

Heather Dawson

THE MUSIC BOX

Rap, pop and punk.
The sound of an elephant's trunk.
Sleaze, beat and sound,
Music is all around.
Tap, jazz and soul,
Rock and roll.
Reggae and heavy-stuff,
Musicians playing until
They're out of puff.
Head-banging and rapping
Sleepyheads caught napping.
Fashion and all the gear,
Different trends - another year.
Nights out. Disco-shout,
Flashing lights
Music, loud. Music, bright.
Whatever music is your trend,
I can honestly recommend
That all good music never dies.
It will always be full of
'Surprise.'

Caroline-Janney

THREE FOUNTAINS

Splatter - splitter - splatter,
High to low - defused.
Splatter - splitter - splatter,
Water ungulates - confused.

Stopping - spluttering - starting,
They splash in differing rhyme.
Yet a unison of caricature,
Set to degrees of time.

Watched by all around,
As in motion they abound.
Three water fountains,
A crescendo in sound.

Gary J Finlay

PLEASURE FOR FREE

I spend many hours watching the sky
seeing the storm clouds rushing by
Sometimes I see a galleon in sail
and then there's a face covered by a veil

Sometimes I see a dog or a cat
Oh no there's a monster
Well who would believe that

So many pictures, so much to see
and the best thing of all
is that this magic is free

Jenny Brownjohn

ESCAPE

Beneath a shady tree
In a lush green, midsummer meadow
Where the grass is prettily punctuated
By simple, random flowers
There is always a soothing spot to sit
And contemplate
When the rest of the world reels and rushes by.

M C Foggin

TWILIGHT YEARS

These, my twilight years
I reminisce on times gone by.
Childhood pranks, fears and tears
But therein lies the wherefore and why's
Of life's maze, of twists, turns and cares.
Twilight of the by and by,
Hopes and ambitions, laid bare,
Before these dimming eyes.

Thoughts that flicker by, like a bird in flight
Or running stream, that is music to the ear.
Fish that scatter in fright,
The gentle cloud that veers,
Hither and thither, before the even-light,
More dreams, more thoughts made clear
In the calm and delight
Of these beautiful twilight years.

Mary Macmillan

HE WAS A CHARACTER!

(Dedicated to my grandad - Manny Shane (Schreiber)

As a comrade once said,
When she knew Manny Schreiber,
Some sixty years ago
'He was a character.'

'Where's 'eh bin?' asks Karla
About her big brother,
When she's an evacuee,
He'd come and rescue her.

To help his wife Yvonne,
Help the war, He got her
A job in industry.
Up at Harris Lebus.

Gaining a BSc
In his fifty-second year,
He went and became
A Civil Engineer.

For his daughter Jacqui,
This caring father,
Of his own business
Became the Guv'ner.

And why am I proud to be,
Manny Shane's grandaughter?
Well, whatever else he's been
He always was a character!

Emma Dorothy Shane

ABORIGINE TREE

Warm colours, too hot for leaves
In the hot sun stands Aborigine tree
Old with the land, by creator's knee
Once lay the small shape of Aborigine tree.

Spirits once known, thin and free
Now lie inside the shelter of Aborigine tree
Old and wise, respected greatly
Is the great twisted form that is Aborigine tree.

May thou survive more years, reaching to me
Your great hospitality Aborigine tree
In the blue climbing sky high as can be
Touching the air Aborigine tree.

The Aborigine tribe worship thee
Mother Nature's creation Aborigine tree
And may you stand tall and proud as you be
Your shape and your body Aborigine tree.

Christopher Johnson (12)

HEART'S DESIRE

He spotted her standing near the window,
she looked so sleek and trim.
He didn't believe in love at first sight,
but she seemed just right for him.
There was richness about her,
a beauty that would not fade.
The kind of perfect model,
to put others in the shade.
She lured him to her side,
allowing him a close inspection.
He would treat her like a lady,
and shower her with affection.
But could she share his life?
At that moment he wasn't sure.
He'd love a chance to take her out,
but would that lead to more?
She was like a professional temptress,
inviting him to sit astride.
His friends would be so envious,
when he took that motorbike for a ride!

Anne Palmer

GETTING TO KNOW THEM

When I first saw them, I knew
They were just what I wanted.
For they had that certain quality about them
So they became a favourite of mine.
I had often thought
That I had put them before anything else.
I found I could not go far without them
As they always accompanied me everywhere I went.
No ifs, no buts, they knew
What was expected of them.
We travelled a lot together
Over many miles we trod.
We were never far apart from each other
Like good old faithful friends.
Then one day it happened.
That was the start of things to come
Which would never be the same again.
Though they have shared their life with me
I tried so hard to avoid that awful question
How much longer will we have together?
Knowing one day we would have to part,
And say goodbye.
But I kept hoping and looking at them
Thinking they didn't look too bad.
Now they sit in a corner in dismay
Just to remind me.
When once, they took the pride and joy in being
The best pair of slippers, I ever had
Are now left, with big holes in their soles.

Lillian Hockley

A SPACEFARER'S SONG

I wish I had a spaceship, so I could fly away.
I'd fly and fly into the sky, in outer space I'd stay.

I'd see the rings of Saturn, and Jupiter's red spot,
On and on past Pluto. See how far I've got!

Asteroids and comets would keep me company,
On and on through space I'd go, to see what I could see.

The triple star of Alpha, and Wolf three-five-nine,
Sirius the dog star, and Barnard's star - just fine.

I'd see the Seven Sisters, and the Great Horse's head.
And Giant Aldebaran, shining bright and red.

Algol the winking demon; clusters, gas clouds, more;
Binaries and systems; and the galactic core.

I wish I had a spaceship, so I could fly away.
I'd fly and fly into the sky, in outer space I'd stay.

The Nebula they call the owl is there for me to see,
And both the Magellanic clouds, and other galaxies.

Canopus, Antares, Procyon Binary,
BD one-six-six-eight, Altair, Aquila - gee!

I wish I had a spaceship, so I could fly away
I'd fly and fly into the sky, in outer space I'd stay.

I wish I had a spaceship, so I could fly away
I'd fly and fly into the sky, in outer space I'd stay.

Athol Cowen

SUNSET

Clouds make way for the sun
Which rises up from hiding
It seems an age since I last saw it
As it rises up whilst brightly shining

Dawn has broken through
The darkness of the night
As I look through the window
At the sun so bright

Slowly it rises
Gleaming upon the world
Like a priceless, precious stone
Or a magnificent pearl

The sky turns yellow
Then orange, then gold
Creating an amazing sight
For the eyes to behold

A moment to treasure
A sight which looks anything but plain
Something so beautiful
You will want to experience it again and again.

Saqib Hussain Malik

TELEPATHIC TED!

I have a lovely teddy bear
whose name is Little John.
I take him with me, everywhere;
- we share a special bond.

I tell him all my troubles;
I tell him all my cares.
I give him lots of cuddles;
- my precious teddy bear.

When my lover, whom I so miss,
cannot be close to me,
I just give Little John my kiss
to send by telepathy!

I hold him close to my heart
so of my thoughts *he* is aware.
Little John is such a smart
and loving teddy bear.

But when I feel sad and glum
my treasured teddy bear
is my also-loved someone;
- exchanging happiness for tears.

Yes, I have a little teddy bear
you could call him my toy boy:
He fills the telepathic air
with my loving thoughts and joy!

Rosemary A V Sygrave

MY BOUQUET OF FLOWERS

I have always loved flowers from a very early age but never had
I imagined holding such a beautiful bouquet.

How very reassuring each flower was given to me in love.
Each having an individual beauty but enhancing each other in a vase.

There are many shapes and sizes and colour range is vast.
The memory of each flower is a treasure in my heart.

Exquisite is the fragrance from each of these delightful blooms
but as their fragrance mingles their sweet perfume fills the room.

How wonderful to see tight buds burst excitedly into bloom and with
their exuberance of youth share their joys and hopes with you.

Other flowers which are part in bloom displaying graceful charm
as their petals unfold revealing softer gentle shades of pale.

But no bouquet would look so gay unless there are some in full array
with dazzling gowns all different shades making life a little brighter
with their colourful displays.

Bubbling over with joy their lilting laughter brings a lightness in
your spirit, you soar on eagles wings.

My bouquet of memories I felt I had to share, for they are my friends
and family who are so very dear.

They have reached out through the years to let people know they care
to quietly come alongside to lend a listening ear.

With love and understanding a tower of strength you will find,
You will know they are God's servants for they go that extra mile.

Each time I walk down memory lane I give a contented smile.
It is because of people like these who make life so worthwhile.

Cecilia Anne Barker

TREES

I watch the trees and see them blow
silver leaves shine and glow.
Walking in a shaded wood
listening to the whispering trees
calling, calling out to me
be happy, be free.
A warmth that is wholly mine
beckons when the sun does shine.
Each and every leaf that falls
tells me soon a new day calls.
Majestic trees when moon time creeps
and silver shadows from hedgerows leap
movements of life, reflections of light
make my heart dance with the night.
I stand and watch the trees in awe
more beauteous than a moonlit shore.
Summer bloom; winter bare; autumn fair;
their blossom fills the springtime air.
No mortal soul should dare to miss
the beauty of eternal bliss.
Leaves of burgundy, leaves of green
leaves of gold and silver seen.
Trees light up my Earthbound heart
when restlessness pulls me apart.
I watch the trees and see them blow
silver leaves shine and glow.

Maureen Hughes

The Rainbow

If I saw a rainbow I would wish that I could see
The crock of gold that waited where the ending ought to be.
For then I could correct the wrongs that make the world so bad and
Dry the tears of heartache that make the undeserving sad.
The homeless and downtrodden, the poor and broken souls
I'd give them all their own small pot of gold.
For the gold is not cash value that would pay a bill or two
But the treasure of contentment granting wishes just for you
Then the blind could see, the deaf could hear, the lonely find a friend
And the crock would last forever, so the joy would never end,
The handicapped would stand up straight, the broken souls would heal,
The homeless would then find a home, the hungry find a meal.
So if you see a rainbow and don't have the time to spend,
Then kindly pass it on to me to follow to its end.

Channon Cornwallis

SUCH ADO ABOUT SOMETHING

The time is retirement
The season is Spring
To freedom, enjoyments
A song with a swing
A watershed waiting
With new things to do
Be proud in creating
What's left there in you
A point of achieving
The ultimate goal
A handshake receiving
Farewell, a new role
For progress is positive
Progress is in place
Let go of what's negative
But keep up the pace!

Norma Anne Macarthur

MAGIC MILLENNIUM MOMENT

Standing on the bridge in night-time's glow,
Where underneath the sparkling water flowed.
You and me in a loving embrace, lost in each other,
From the crowds we escaped.
They all walk by but we were going somewhere,
And I swear at that moment we were the only ones there.
Drifting away I like the river below, we shared tonight with others,
This moment was ours to let go.

Martyn Howells

LOUDER THAN WORDS

The best things in life, we're told, are free
Then please could you explain to me
Why we're running around, chasing our tails,
Depending on the state when all else fails,
Grabbing, grasping, 'What about me?'
Stress and rage are all we see.
Can't we shout 'Stop', calm down, get wise.
Can't we learn to open our eyes,
Be aware, look around, blink and see
The best things in life truly are free.

How do I know? Well it's like this
I've discovered the joy there is in a kiss,
In a hug or a cuddle that we call affection
To others it gives us a bond, a connection.
The sticky kiss of a grandchild small,
The hug from a son now so tall.
Now I have a new, added bliss
The rather unexpected, passionate kiss
Of a new, late partner with eyes just for me,
The best things in life are truly for free.

Jay Hemmings

MY RIVER

It's spring down by the river,
There's a gentle happy charm,
It glides along in restful peace,
Smooth and flat and calm.

The water has a sparkle,
As the sun shines through the trees
There's a small white wave, a ripple
Started by the summer breeze.

Further down, just round the bend,
At first you hear the grumble,
It's autumn now, the water's high
You see it jump and tumble.

Now winter's here and from the moor
Large bits of trees and bushes
Float down and choke the grey stone bridge
As the river roars and rushes.

The river's moods, in rain or shine
Are exciting, grave or gay,
It's comforting to know it's there
And busy every day.

Enid Gill

BLUE

The colour of sky
Maybe waves upon the shore
Sometimes a blonde's eye
But I see it more and more.

Maybe it's your wall
It might even be your door
It could be your hall
And I see it more and more.

Forget-me-not shade
Crocuses in their full bloom
They come to spring's aid
Beautiful, glorious, blue.

Sarah Cresswell

FOUR DIMENSIONS OF BEING

The life of the body brings pleasure
But that's not an end in itself.
The life of the mind brings wisdom
Do not keep it all on the shelf.

The life of the spirit brings love and devotion
And union with the divine.
The life of the soul is eternal
Where peace and light ever shine.

Martin Harvey

BEARS

Let me have one, Daddy
I will love him
and tell him stories
about bad bears who
live in dark green woods
and tumble about
on beds of
pine needles and brown leaves.
He will love me,
and follow me to the bottom
of our garden
and watch me when I play
in my sandpit.
I will call him Alphonse.

A L Griffin

POETRY IS MY PLEASURE

What pleasure or message do we find hidden
in the rhyme or verse of a poem?
So many can we find when we spend our
leisure time, with our head deep in a book.
Read on, let's take a look.

When reading Wordsworth's, 'Lucy Gray',
only just the other day, the message was
plain and clear.
Hold your children dear and never let
them stray, love them with all your heart
less they fade away.

Rudyard Kipling too, brings a strong message to you.
In his wonderful poem, 'If', is contained a
message for life. Quote,
If you can keep your head when all about you
are losing theirs and blaming it on you.
Those awe-inspiring lines carry a message
for all time.

At the Last Night of the Proms you will
always hear this song.
Penned by William Blake, 'Jerusalem',
brings my soul awake. Quote,
And was the Holy Lamb of God
On England's pleasant pastures seen?

Whatever new message you're looking for,
you may find it deep in the oil of life.
In the wonderful words of a poem.
Old or new there are poems waiting to be
discovered by you, so read on and enjoy.

Robert Waggitt

NASA

NASA has a few main projects at present,
One is the International Space Station sounding pleasant,
It's being constructed with three parts very slowly,
Whilst the Mars Global Surveyor Programme's treated holy.
The sun's being explored by a monitoring satellite,
A small scale prototype of the Skippy space flight;
The Hyper Soar spaceplane and other planetary exploration,
Beyond our solar system is all expanding information.
Out of the space shuttle, International Space Station,
Concorde and Hyper Soar spaceplane of any nation;
The spaceplane is the longest size of four,
The space shuttle had the widest size score.
The space shuttle is the fastest in speed,
When it reaches the main cut off need;
And Concorde is flown from UK's international airports,
Every decade millions of passenger need more courts.
Requirements are more runways added onto all airports,
Expensive holidays, outside stands built for all sorts;
Of waiting at and getting onto supersonic planes,
Away from terminal gates multiplying in bought lanes.
British Aerospace are developing the airbus family aft,
Military transport, supersonic and six hundred seater aircraft,
Whilst I develop artwork for the space station's use,
I sent NASA's notices, poetry and drawings loose.

Ian K A Ferguson (B A Hons)

CHRISTMAS CARDS

The trees are a greenness, a greyness, a silver,
In a white, whizzing whirl of delirious glitter.
The houses - a wonder of old-fashioned world,
With bright orange windows and welcoming ways.

The horses are prancing and preening and pawing,
Carriages careening along with the crowd.
Urchins a'carolling, calling and capering,
Dancing around with abandon untamed.

Gentlefolk muffled in warm woollen clothing,
Dawdling yet dandified, greeting their kind.
Church in the background, extolling the virtues
Of Christ born forever - the Saviour of Souls.

Margaret Kellman

BEST THINGS IN LIFE

The best things in life are captured in our fantasies
as they do not happen as often as I would hope it to be,
but maybe this is just the reason, why some things which
happen only in a captured moment seem so perfect.

It's that feeling that bubbles in your tummy, and makes
you feel warm inside, it's like someone above wants to
give you some love, and sends it in a form of good luck.
The best things in life are the gifts that are not forgotten
but surround us every day.

To many the best things in life are those wishes which
give the permission to escape from the fabric folds of the
workplace, unloving relationships and pain. Just to
imagine the flowing fields of green, the petals so pretty it
makes life gleam, return to reality and all seems bare
but the best things in life exist.

The feeling of falling in love, so deep, surely is one of the
best things which you can keep, and every time he looks
in your eyes you know deep inside that all the best things
are linked to love, so when you think of the best
things in your life I bet it's a memory you have in your
heart, which makes you lucky, as all the best things in
life will be yours to hold on for.

Sarah Ewing

LIFE'S MEASURE

If I can look and see,
Yet not perceive;
Listen and hear,
But rarely understand;
Should I experience
But scarcely feel;
Or like exceedingly -
But never love;
Or music please my ear
But never thrill my soul;
Fine words inform my mind,
But fail to reach my heart;
I have not lived,
But pallidly existed.
The glory missed -
A heaven not attained.
Letting life pass me by,
So fearful of the depths
Where wonder waits
Just for the taking.

Mary Pledge

THE TRUE STORY OF MY BROTHER, PAUL

I have a favourite brother
And his first name is Paul.
But I'm afraid to say he has just one fault;
He's just mad about *football!*
It would take a dozen servants
His clothes to wash and scrub,
If Paul became a member
Of his favourite football club.

I have a favourite brother
And his first name is Paul.
But I'm afraid to say he has just one fault;
He likes that *roar!*
He's just adopted a lion
That he hasn't even seen,
Dad's mad about the price
I can see what he means.

I have a favourite brother
And his first name is Paul.
But I'm afraid to say he has just one fault;
He drove in the *hall!*
I'm sure you see the faults in that,
I mean he was only twelve
But there is little we could do,
Except listen to Mum yell.

I have a favourite brother
And his first name is Paul.
But I'm afraid to say he has just *one* fault;
He's driving us up the wall!
But he's still my favourite brother because he's so interesting,
How many of you have a brother who has
wonaspittingcontestortapdancedwhileeatingamelon and
                                        speaks Mandarin.

Yubing Zhu

MY GAME

I loved to sit upon the grass
and gaze up to the sky.
I play a game called 'What is that'.
As the clouds go slowly by
you see the shapes of different
things, how wonderful they are,
a rabbit with a fluffy tail,
a bird that flies so far.
The clouds they are so magical up
there in the sky, they're just like
cotton fields as I lay here
and see them roll by.

Jenna Cook (11)

YEARS AGO

The branches slouch overhead,
An oppressive storm appears to hang.
The wizened trunks, able to tell a thousand tales,
Lean attentively towards the river

As it lazily meanders by.
It's glistening, bronze surface licks
The soft, sandy banks on which we stand,
Reflecting all we see above.

The mosquitoes pass us, a shimmer of
Heat on a sticky summer's day,
Beginning their jaunty dance
As if puppets on a string,

Taunting the very things we strain for.
We've been standing here for a while now,
Yet hope and high spirits still rustle the almost
Silent, whispering leaves above us.

It is the thought of what we can't see that excites us.

Neil Curry

LET LOOSE

There was once a band,
A far superior band to any other,
'Let Loose' they were called.
Richie, Rob and Lee,
My favourite band, superb singers, superb performers,
Top 10 hits they did have,
In concert excellently superb.
Richie Wermerling, the lead singer, what a hunk, *wow*.
Rob Jeffrey, the guitarist, blonde dreamboat.
Lee Murray, the drummer, really nice guy.
I met them four times, really, really nice they were.
My favourite band now split up but always remembered,
They brought out the best in me, take it easy
I'm crazy for you,
I wish I were their one night stand
And make it with you.
I wish Richie was mine, my darling be home soon.
My arm I got Richie to sign, then later tattooed in,
He saw, he was amazed,
He always said, 'Hi there' after when we met he knew me.
I hope one day they'll perform together again soon.
Until then hope they appear solo.
I love 'Let Loose' - the greatest band
In the world.

Michelle Knight

ODE TO AN OCTOGENARIAN

Our Olive has served the Messingham Pensioners for twenty-five years.
She always stood out among her peers
This surely cannot go without recognition
Even though this was not without repetition
At first the meetings were held in the Co-op community hall
In those days there were thirty-eight members
Thursday afternoons have always been meeting days
When everyone tried to mend their ways
Each meeting began with a hymn
This was followed by the Lord's Prayer
After this a guest speaker or group of singers
And even sometimes a group of handbell ringers
Entertained the whole group for about forty-five minutes
The singers sung like linnets
Our Olive always auctioned the produce that was given
She always tried to get as much as possible
Each meeting concluded with a tea
This included sandwiches, cakes and plum bread
This cheered everyone up and they chatted together
Some of Olive's faithful flock went on holiday
This was enjoyed by one and all
It included workouts for all the girls
In their bedrooms in the morning instead of doing their curls
The meeting them moved to the chapel
The same procedure was followed
In 1981 our village hall was opened
To fund all these meetings the monthly jumble sale took place
This was time consuming but still enjoyed by all
Tea and biscuits were to follow
To help fill those tummies for ever hollow

P Boult

FRIENDS AND FAMILY

My friends and family are the best things in my life,
I don't know what I'd do without them,
They care,
And share,
My mum makes my tea,
And my friends play with me,
I have a good time with my friends,
My friendship with them will never end,
When my friends come to my house,
They're always as quiet as a mouse,
My mum and dad make them laugh,
My friends probably think they're daft,
I sometimes play board games with my mum,
And I think they're a lot of fun,
I sometimes play computer games with my dad,
But I lose so I get mad,
My friends and family make a good team,
None of them are nasty or mean,
My friends and family are the best,
They're better than any of the rest.

Danielle Croud

GREY BEAR

I had a toy bear called 'Grey Bear'
He was a bear of wisdom and grace
A bear both loving and tender
In whom a child's trust could be placed

My Grey Bear was faithful and friendly
He saw my tears and helped nurse me through
He was always the first there to cheer me
Oh little Grey Bear I loved you

When life as an adult gets tougher
Problems beset every side
I know that even if things get much rougher
I can turn to the grey bear inside

I had a bear called 'Grey Bear'
A bear of wisdom and grace
A bear both fun loving and wondrous
In whom this child's trust has been placed

Mark S Williams

ALL THAT'S BEST IN LIFE TO ME

(For Molly Ann)

Well Molly Ann at last, you'd kept us hanging loose
And now we're all a panic with what we have to do
I got the call, 'OK dear I'll be there soon as I can.'
I drove the streets through London, avoided every jam.

I sped into the car park then rushed off through the wards
I puffed at every stairway and clambered through swing doors
'Hello,' I said, 'I'm Gurney.' The nurse showed me the door
My little Molly Ann, was there to take the floor.

They'd ironed out all the wrinkles, your skin as smooth as silk
Your hair like straw all shiny, your eyes were blue as well
You lay there quite contented a smile formed on your lips
At last our little treasure of what life has to give.

You hardly made a whimper when sleeping through the day
But often made your protests through the night to our dismay
Well Mummy gave a cuddle and brought you to the breast
And soon were all back sleeping and getting hard earned rest.

Well time goes by so quickly and soon you're out for play
We'll toss aside the rattles, there for another day
Well what about the music box, OK a cuddly toy
OK you want my spectacles, Oh Molly you're a joy.

It's six months now, you're teething and not a pretty sight
All red around the cheeks and noisy through the night
Your grisly through the day and very hard to please
But little Molly Gurney, you're all that's best in life to me.

Raymond David Gurney

MOONRISE

I gazed across the darkened sky,
Lo and behold before my very eyes,
Peeping over the houses and looking my way,
Was the moon arising in such bright array?
Slowly but surely it steadily rose
Taking only seconds to turn day into night,
To light up the clouds all silvery bright,
Then the full moon took up its pose
Shining in glory for everyone to see.
What amazing joy it gave to me,
Nature what wonder and pleasure,
The lovely moments for me to treasure.

Evelyn M Harding

MY HOLY BIBLE

My best friend is my Holy Bible
With its contents of everlasting
Forgiveness, though I have been a rebel
In times gone by, but God's heavenly
                              bells did ring

Though battles did rage in the old book
God tested His people to the limit
But He took them back to His heavenly nook
He blessed them and made them spiritually fit

The second book in my Holy Bible
Depicts our Lord Jesus Christ
A sinless man portrayed as a common rebel
Yet, He was the Son of God, the perfect prophet

This wonderful book I read every day
I believe in its contents
In every possible way
Glory be to God and Jesus who rents His life
                              for us all

My Holy Bible I will treasure for the rest of my life
Even though it is becoming rather battered
I'll mend it forever, God's gift
To me, His hopeful Christian who is most
                              thankfully flattered

Alma Montgomery Frank

MY CHILDREN

What is a child, but a gift from God to share our love,
a sheer miracle from heaven
conceived, born, and above
the mysteries of mankind no one can deny
the beauty in a child
the innocence they imply.
They torture us with tantrums
then climb upon our knee;
their little arms caress our neck
then, kiss us passionately.
They sometimes drive us to despair
and so to bed is bliss;
but when they're sick or far away
their love we're sure to miss.
Their childhood days pass much too quick
those games we used to play;
such memories we can't erase . . .
for adults they are today.

Margaret R Bevan

NELL

Nell loves me . . .
> All the days, despite my ways
> > Nell loves me . . .

Time you cheat
> When you defeat
> > and cast me to eternity . . .
> Say I grew old . . .
> > That I grew sad . . .
> > > That fame and wealth
> > They passed me . . .

But then you fraud,
> You'll have to add . . .
> > Nell loved me!

Anthony O Wilkinson

HEIDI AND HOLLY

Heidi and Holly go out to play,
Oh! It is such a beautiful day.
To run and chase the rabbits gay,
What fun it is to play and play.

We love our pussies to us so kind,
What pleasures they are to hold
in the mind.

So be free great creatures to roam
and roam,
But always come back to us
at your home.

Mairi Thornhill

MY WHIM

I have this whim
To write a poem.

I have this urge
To join the surge,
And be a part
Of this current art.

I have to go
With the flow,
To join the mob
And do this job.

I have to see
If this is me,
And I have words
To join the herds.

To write my lines,
Be with the times.

Adrienne Price

MY FAVOURITE THINGS

My favourite thing must be my life,
So why waste time with tears and strife?
You only have one life to live,
Don't be a taker be one that gives.

There's so many wonderful things on Earth,
The flowers and the sunshine and the miracle of birth.
Even the insects we don't like,
They too have the right to live their life.

It's a wonderful world we live in you know.
Like the mountains on high and the rivers that flow
Into the sea to reach far off lands,
While on your journey lend a helping hand.

Each season of the year has their wonderful sights,
In spring the awakening of winter's dark nights.
The garden comes alive with flowers that say,
'God bless you Mum' on Mother's Day.

Spring turns to summer with days by the sea,
Lazing on the beach is where you'll find me.
The autumn arrives and we kick through the leaves,
That lay on the ground from the sad looking trees.

The invention of TV and the compact disc
Is one I'm glad I didn't miss.
How sad that people in days gone by couldn't enjoy
Listening to Sir Cliff and Danny Boy, (O'Donnell).

Make the most of your life however humble,
Never mind if people grumble,
On your face always wear a smile
For we're only on this Earth for a very short while.

Yvonne Lewis

WE'LL NEVER FIND A BETTER WAY

Tall in the saddle, legs take the strain.
Fresh air and freedom, so much physical gain.

Peace and contentment, so much to see.
Take a good look, this is the real me.

Your heart is the engine, your legs to propel.
Setting wheels in motion, animal and mineral gel.

Not a sign of pollution, little congestion.
If you know of something better, I'll take the suggestion.

It's the in thing in China but that's not where it ends.
There's Holland the flat lands and the East Anglian fens.

Always convenient, your velocipede friend.
Its workings are feasible, so that you can comprehend.

The cycle is so efficient, where can you find
Such a marvellous way, of moving mankind?

T A Napper

AWAKE IN THE DARK

A little voice, a little cry,
A little tear forms in her eye.
'Mummy!' calls her little voice.
A little sob the only noise
That carries down the stairs:
Up I go, taking them in pairs.

My poor love, my little girl,
My little angel, my life's pearl.
My little girl in Mummy's bed,
Looking for her sleepy head.
No-one's there! Where's Mummy gone?
Pillow empty, light's not on!

It's alright love, Mummy's here,
Never far, always near.
Washing-up and clearing away
Have kept me from my bed again!
Hugs and cuddles, reassure,
Hugs and cuddles, plenty more!

At long last the work is done,
And back to bed goes little one.
Another hug, another story,
A special kiss, just for me.
Goodnight my love, and in your sleep
Safe and warm your dreaming keep.

Kathryn J Hayward

LITTLE HAMPTON

Sun, shine forth on me, I beg you
Desperate and hungry
I need divine love but my lover's far away
And I'm living in faith
Crying for that divine touch
My source of lasting patience
Stay on with me, I only plead

Sitting by the English Sea
You respect no one
And so I cling to you
But one thing is clear
Your breath is hot and I'm melting away
All my misfortunes

My little friend dances to Cuban music
'O' why for it brings back memories
Remembering my first dance
I can always relate to that I thought

The young man has an inch of humour
A little like yours
More of the past I see
But baby, I'm musing still
It's all part of my future
A precious past well to drink on.

Roza Ajibola

A Precious Memory

The best thing in my life
Is a memory
Which I will treasure forever
As I'm really sure it was meant
Just for me, only me
And to tell you about it I'll now endeavour.

One night in bed
As I stared at the moon
I prayed for our *Lord* to hear me
And come to me sometime soon.

I then experienced a feeling
A glorious exciting one
It enveloped me in a warmth.
As warm as the midday sun.

God was with me that night.
Listening to me.
Comforting me I know.

Something precious
Had taken place then
Which I shall never forget
And so
If this is the atmosphere in heaven
We still have a much better life
To pray for.
And for us all to look forward to yet.

Patricia Harrison

THE SUNSET OF THE SEASON

Autumnal sunset brings to its close
this luminous day. Soft the air, only
gently rippling waves disturb the stillness.

Between lake and woodland beech trees now are
almost bare, a symphony of white grey black
etched against sky's quiet colouring
whilst those few leaves still clinging like
golden coins to the upper boughs, are reflected
in the water. Sentinel seagulls on a line of
stakes witness the journeying of moorhens.

Two wanderers through glades rain-soaked and
carpeted with leaf-fall, pause by a willow
felled by winter storms; as was the silvery
beech, now resting in another's sisterly
embrace. Once they had heard its lament
as the wind teased at its wounds.

As the sun declines, its image, as theirs
mirrored in transparent waters, both silently
share in the wonder, intuitive of poised
fragility of peace, its closeness to loss.

Never less sweet, the memory.

Louise Rogers

FRIENDS FOREVER!

The best thing in my life would have to be my friend,
The fun we always have just never seems to end.
We go to the town and even the clubs,
We're not old enough *yet* to get into pubs!
She always knows when I'm down,
And wipes off my sad little frown.
We've stuck together through good and bad,
What a friendship we certainly have.
I think I'm the luckiest girl on Earth,
To have such a friendship, since our birth.
We've known each other for so very long,
And our friendship has just kept growing strong.
People say our friendship is forever,
I hope they're right because this friendship, I do treasure.
I'd give up anything just to stay friends,
If our straight path begins to bend.
This friendship we have is the best thing to me,
I'm glad we're friends and friends we will always be.

Kimberley Rushforth

A TRIP TO THE ZOO

An extra day's holiday, so what shall we do?
The weather is fine, take a trip to the zoo
Paying the entrance fee, we walk in the grounds
To be greeted by a chorus of many strange sounds

The 'King of the Jungle', the lion sits with pride
Whilst amongst the foliage, the snow leopard does hide
The camels look magnificent, oh one is trying to sit
Please keep your distance, these animals will spit

My favourite the zebra, like a horse in striped pyjamas
Their every move being watched, by the inquisitive llamas
We all gather round, to see the elephants being fed
A weird sucking feeling, as their trunk takes the bread

The monkeys are going crazy, really acting the fool
Whilst the seals swim around, trying to keep cool
Penguins looking like little waiters, waddling about
In the distance, the parrots start to scream and shout

Elegant flamingos are sunbathing by the lake
The rhinoceros is wallowing, his mudbath does take
Giraffes munching the treetops, their favourite dish
Whilst the keeper is feeding, the otters with fish

Then to the reptile house, to see many a snake
The alligator stirs and is suddenly awake
The iguana is fascinating as we come face to face
Against the glass his foot, to my hand he does place

So unhappy are the tigers as they pace up and down
Whilst in the trees the lemur, happily swing around
The brown bear comes over, to give us a glance
Attention seeking, looks like he's trying to dance

It's now time to go, it's been a magical day out
We'll be sure to visit again, there is no doubt

Linda Brown

MY FATHER

A father is love
A father is very special
Not like a mother -
Different but just as important.
Cherished, childhood memories
Of giggling, fun bathtimes,
Of playing special father games,
Walks in the country hand-in-hand,
Making sandcastles on a seaside beach,
And games, many games of tennis and cricket.
Christmases spent together - a family round the
$\qquad\qquad\qquad\qquad\qquad$ Christmas tree
Opening presents with the crackling and tearing noises
$\qquad\qquad\qquad\qquad\qquad$ as the paper is ripped off.
And -
As you grow into adulthood talks about growing up
Sharing secrets that only your father can share with you
Memories that do not fade
Even unto death
Memories that will remain crystal clear into eternity.
And then, when death separates you
You know that is when you become especially close
And walk together through life with God into the unknown.
Thank you Dad.

Margaret Smith

SOLDIER BOY

Get ready to serve your country,
The last document has been signed,
You've got your marching orders,
So leave that rock and roll music behind.

Your hair is considered too long,
So Memphis boy be brave,
After your medical,
Your quiff is in for a shave.

You're in the army now,
It will make your mother proud,
Dressed in your US uniform,
You're now just one of the crowd.

Germany is beckoning,
It's time to meet your ploy,
It's going to be tough,
For a singing soldier boy.

Debbie Twine

A FAITHFUL PET

Who can forget a faithful pet,
That has left this world behind?
Now and again a memory,
Will spring into your mind.

The playful times and happy hours,
Which you and your dog shared.
The love and trust she gave to you,
Because you always cared.

Your every mood was noted,
By this faithful canine friend,
And she was so devoted,
Right to the end.

Her golden coat so silky,
And eyes so shining bright.
Your pal and your protection,
Now gone from your sight.

The joy she gave to you in life,
So many hours of pleasure.
Are thoughts which you will cling to,
Memories you will treasure.

Whether animal or human,
Love is the strongest tie.
So say, 'Farewell, 'til we meet again.'
Never say goodbye.

M Wakefield

A Walk In The Country

Have you ever wandered through a wood
With trees that stretch to the sky?
Have you ever walked in knee length corn
And seen a purple butterfly?

There's rabbits in all the fields
And ants that make their nest below.
White swans that float along the river
Beside the fields where flowers grow.

I've heard a nightingale in song,
I've seen a water rat at large,
Mother Nature grows them all
And everyone is free of charge.

Georgina Waite

THINGS I LOVE

So many things I love;
Warm sunshine, bright blue skies, cloud-patterned,
Pigeons cooing, buzzards mewing as they soar aloft,
Ravens croaking,
Scent of new-baked bread
And of ploughed fields after rain,
Fulfilled cackle of hens,
Twittering of swallows,
Spring's first delicate flowers and tender green
Of burgeoning leaves.
Feel of fresh air blowing on my face,
Raindrops splashing my cheek,
Taste of sun-warmed fruits
And new-dug potatoes,
A cat's contented purr, a blackbird's song,
A shower of summer roses,
Warm fragrance of ripening blackberries
And of fresh-mown grass,
Music of running streams
And cries of sheep and lambs and chattering rooks
And far-off pheasant call,
The gale's thunder,
The sea's roar,
The gulls' excited screams . . .

These, and many, many more, speak to my senses
And make me rejoice to be alive in this wonderful world
Where only man's cruelty is grievous . . .

Evelyn Scott Brown

MY TEDDY BOO

Many teddy bears I have known
Most in my childhood years
When Mum gave all mine to a jumble sale
I must admit I shed a few tears

Then one day when out at the shops
A special one caught my eye
I couldn't go home without him
I knew I just had to buy

He's been with me now for many years
So looking the worse for wear
We've travelled together all over the world
Me and my teddy bear

He's never very far from me
Especially when I'm asleep
I've given many things away
But my Teddy Boo I'll always keep

Mary Lunn

TIDAL LARGESS

Strolling along the beach
with crunching stride, pausing
to explore the shoreline of ebbing tide.
Half buried treasures revealed
by relinquishing waves -
crevice glimpsed, leading to brine etched cave.

I inhale deeply, salty breath of the sea
and sweet content, meanders with me.
Curious seagulls, shout their pleasure in the day,
while I delve into bounty, from tidal sway.
Lone yacht catches the breeze, together they flirt and tease -
beachcombing now among the rocks, I pause to watch . . .

Joanne Manning

CURLEW HAVEN

Where seagulls scream and curlews cry
an osprey pauses on a post
watching over seaweed crust
for his prey.

Where onshore breezes bluster by
and distant hills are grey in mist
nature's curious peace is dressed
in serenity.

The sudden sight of clouds and fowl
of sun on water in the bay
is such an overriding joy
and peace withal

and we would leave our day undone
to stand where seabirds wheel and cry
inhabiting the estuary
sharing the boon.

Sally Grey

MIRACLE OF BIRTH

The miracle when your newborn first you hold,
The richest blessing - more precious than gold,
The tiny downy head on your breast lays,
The happy loving feeling to fill all your days.

The wondrous feeling is like no other,
The miracle and joy when first you are a mother,
The tiny form you press close to your heart,
The bond you share - no one can tear apart.

And as the years go by and quickly they grow,
You love and gently guide them as best you know,
In return they give you joy not like any other,
Oh what a wonderful miracle to be a mother!

Doris Thordarson

THE MAGIC YOU DO

I delve deep inside to find
an excuse to reason all the doubt out
of my mind about you.
As I take a microscopic view
at your life,
and all the things that you do.
For you take a little bit of this and
you take a lot of that.
Oh you pull my heart right out
like a rabbit from a hat.
Yes that's the magic you do
and I can't help but fall in love with you.
No, I can't help but fall in love with you.

D G Morgan

GRANNY'S CURTAINS

The spare room's been repainted now,
The walls are fresh and clean,
I've hung bright pictures on them
And the paint is apple-green.

The floor is polished and re-stained,
The carpet washed and swept,
I've made new cushion covers,
But something I have kept . . .

Granny's curtains, daisy-sprigged,
With roses intertwining,
Of dainty cotton, tiny-stitched,
And finest, soft white lining.

She gave them to my mother,
Who passed them on to me;
They're still as sweet as ever,
And beautiful to see.

In my very early days,
In my own room she drew
Those curtains on my window
When the pale moonlight shone through.

And when our baby's born next year,
(I hope we'll have a girl),
She'll lie and watch those curtains
As in the breeze they twirl.

My friends don't understand me;
'Nylon washes with such ease,
You can choose so many patterns
That cannot fail to please.'

I stick to Granny's curtains,
Though faded now in part,
They brighten still the bedroom,
And a corner in my heart.

Sylvia Herbert

SEA MYSTERY

Scene of wild delight and homely fun
In summer; then deserted, unrewarded
Windswept turmoil of summers past and gone;
Alone save the faithful seagulls, who
With the Creator share the eternal and sublime
Secret of this grey-green monster,
Washing, washing the age-old shores of time.
Your slow, seething waves, shifting
The lazy shingle and stubborn sand of centuries
Past and gone, draw me to sleep, drifting
On your foamy back like leaves in a stream.
No, you can never be tamed. You will go on, so
Defying the rules that man has obeyed
Since Time first started on his ceaseless journey.
Men must die and thus they go,
But you roll on, so slow, so slow.

Martin Winbolt-Lewis

TOMMY THE HORSE

Of the Riding School horses I love one the best,
For me he's superior to all of the rest.
And today I'm especially happy because
I am to ride Tommy my favourite horse.
When out of his box Tommy is led,
His coat is rich chestnut, the ruddiest red,
I cannot but think as he's given to me
How handsome he is. What nobility.
So up on his back I softly spring
Ready to join the rest of the string
Tommy he's happy his wits all about,
I'm certain he knows that he's going out.
We walk through the gate, through the field to the lane
Where rabbits are playing they're *chase me* game
Then out of a walk, into a trot,
Tommy is dancing, clippety clop.
We overtake walkers where the path turns the bend
'Hello, I'm Tommy and this is my friend.'
Then down to the end of the ridge we travel.
We then turn for home and I feel I'm in trouble
For Tommy says 'Hey for a canter I'm ready'
'Now Tommy' say I 'you've got to go steady,'
And just when we settle on a reasonable pace
Tommy again thinks that he's in a horse race
But a touch on his rein and he slackens his speed,
Oh Tommy you are such a sweet tempered steed.
Only one canter more and it's off for home,
Tommy is certain his job was well done,
Oh Tommy you are such a wonderful horse,
And if you were mine, well you're not of course
But when I'm at home, I can always consider
That Tommy was mine, at least for an hour.

Joan Robson

WORDS FROM HER HEART

Singing a song her voice did drift, as she sat there
shedding tears.
No one heard her music, alone for many years.
One day she took a pen and then begun to write.
Hours she spent using words, teaching herself to fight.
The ink laid down on paper, she hoped to be discovered,
For although she hid behind a pen, her depth was now uncovered.
Happy and alone no more, for her heart on paper spilled.
Gone was the life she had before, as the words her heart they filled.

Vicki Michele Loveday

MY SWEETHEART

I think the best thing in my life
was the day I met my loving wife
With bright blue eyes and yellow hair
to me a beauty beyond compare

She spoke to me in a friendly way
and with her charm she made my day
We gaily chatted as we walked along
my attraction for her became quite strong

I made a date for a theatre show
and was elated when she agreed to go
From that time on within my heart
I knew I'd found my true sweetheart

Soon we were both engaged to wed
then the banns were being read
We have been married many years
and divorce has never been a fear

Lachlan Taylor

MY OWN BACKYARD ...

I'd travelled all around the world
What was I searching for?
I searched for unconditional love,
but I found none at all.
Returned home, my strength depleted,
there sat in my backyard.
'Twas there I found the treasure
I'd been searching for so hard.
I saw treasures in the blossoms,
and in every leaf and tree.
Saw love's majestic beauty,
a gift to such as me.
I learned I'd travelled with no sight,
had sought but could not find.
Love I could not recognise
for I was more than sightly blind.
Thought everything quite pointless
when love had a meet with me.
He opened up so many doors
the day He let me see . . .

Rosie Hues

HEAVEN FOR ME

From a point atop the steps
Which lead on down toward the bay
I wondered at the ocean
On a bright November day
At the oft so strong and stormy sea
All puddled in placidity
As it washed its peace on over me
And blew my blues away

As I stopped there in that perfect place
My eyes turned to the sky
Where from light bright blue and bright white cloud
I saw a seagull fly
And I marvelled as this oft maligned
Bird swooped in front then wheeled behind
Then in language man will never find
Called to me with its cry

So I really do not care
At others ridiculing me
For the telling of my thoughts about
These things they do not see
And it matters not if the sun is bright
If a fog rolls in, if the stars give light
Or if a tempest howls with ungodly might
This place
Is Heaven
For me

Andy Scott

TO A BLACK RABBIT

Black with one white patch
And two white gloves.
Two tall white ears
And whiskers poised.
You sit ever watchful,
Hopeful of human company
And a frolic inside
On the big carpet meadow.
Pleased by so little -
Warmth, food and shelter,
But most of all love.
Love that has extended
Your life to ripe old age.
Never knowing the outside world -
Meadows, fields and forests.
To run and burrow
And meet your mates,
But cushioned in safety
In a straw-lined hutch,
Away from preying owls,
Cunning stealthy foxes,
And next door's demonic cat.
You are much loved
And have given much pleasure.

Maree S Speakman

SNOW ON TREES

Swirling, silent, flakes of snow,
Drifting downwards, fast, then slow.
Settling softly on each tree,
A white gold shape of filigree.
Each tree a jewel in its own right,
Retains its beauty through the night.
That master craftsman, morning sun,
Highlights each jewel, one by one.
Nature's mantle, soft and white,
Transforms each tree for our delight.

J D Robertson

PRICELESS

From the moment we first met, it was like
we were meeting again.
And from that time we both knew we'd
have a friendship we can't explain.

We never had no big secrets or past distant
times to share
It's as though every lifetime experience, we
each had, we were both there

We have a special understanding that's
very rare and unique
'Shall I be Mother?' one is always strong
if the other is feeling weak.

But we are individuals with minds
of our own
And although we're surrounded by
loved ones - we both felt alone.

Mandie Lester

SHARING MY PERSONAL TREASURE

There's one treasure in the world, of which I really care,
A gift that I'd not throw away, but I'd always share,
That's the product of my writing, in poetic form,
As I escape the real world, in both night and morn.

My imagination, and life's experiences too,
Help formulate a poem, that others may like to view,
And hope the finished product, gives pleasure in its lines,
As much as I've found enjoyment, in my verse and rhymes.

I love the time when I escape, and I pen a verse,
Forgetting problems in the world, that are far much worse,
In places of disasters, of plague, and flood, and drought,
I find my inner mind, and seek a poetic sprout.

That grows and grows within the words, of my inner mind,
Allowing me to capture, ideas that I find,
To bring them on to paper, in a poetic rhyme,
Expanding my first idea, into every line.

I ask for understanding, I shall not give away,
My very special treasure, of which I love and pray,
Will give me great enjoyment, as days and weeks go by,
Helping me within my life, of which time seems to fly.

Nigel Lloyd Maltby

BORNE ON THE BREEZE

Can you hear the sound of music
Wafting through the trees?
Like violins and soft guitars
Conducted by the breeze.
Every now and then you'll hear
Accompanying the strings
A magic voice somewhere near
Of a little bird that sings.

The night is dark but the moon is bright
Casting shadows all around,
It seems they're dancing, fairy-light
Scarce touching on the ground.
Swaying, bending to the music
That's wafting through the trees,
With a pirouette and a graceful kick
Such artistry must please.

No longer is the sound of music
Wafting through the trees.
My heart is sad, my soul is sick
For ugly sounds are these.
There's the wail from a warning siren
There are police and firemen too
And the raucous sounds of cars and men
Descending from the blue

I sigh, my magic moment fades
I turn to wander home
I still can see the dancing shades
Of the shadows as I roam.
But wait! all is not lost, for once again
A chorus of song I hear
And it seems to me to be quite plain
That the spirit of peace draws near.

Kathleen Holmes

LOVE'S VISION

Oh we have touched the heart of love. This is
Love and in loving still do these lips kiss
Those sweet shadows where your memory is.
Cleopatra and her Antony, Ronsard
Or young Romeo, Heloise and Aberlard -
We are their peers. With no greater wonder
Did they upon their lovers' lips wreak plunder.
Our souls like theirs in beauty yielded then
Never to be their own in loneliness again.
As sun brings flowers when winter's nearly done,
As moon draws gently on a tide that's just begun,
We could not then nor can discover now
What blessed vision touched us, nor how
This love in which our lives as jewels are set
Like calmest water in some coign of the land inlet
Puts all earth, all matchless beauty in our debt.

Uvedale Tristram

THE EVENING LIGHT

Subdues each day
to mellow tones,
as the sun completes its arc;
iridescent hues
of subtle form
merge the daylight into dark.

The crescent moon
outshines the sun,
and mocks its fading beam;
so blanched and bold
reflecting cold
the sunset's golden gleam.

And insects dance
in the slanting rays
of evening's haloed light;
as an early owl
begins its call,
to advance the coming night.

When the final hour
has reached its close,
light no longer domineers;
though myriad stars
opaque and glazed,
shower the sky with sequined tears.

Susan Turner

LIGHT OF OUR LIFE

With words I'm nothing special
Sometimes not knowing what to say
Although they are not poetic
They're meant in every way

The smile on your face
Portrays it all
Today we both feel ten feet tall
Tears in my eyes are only of joy
Today you gave birth to our baby boy.

Charles Bevill Warcup

OCCIDENCE

Still now I warm to that autumnal equinox,
As the envoy of evening crept into the ember horizon,
Embraced by the celestial patience of diurnal occultation,
Whilst the heliacal setting fragments the crystallisation of night
Envious of amber
I learned how to burn.

Anthony John Ward

I CRIED!

I cried!
For John Lennon!
I cried!
For Linda McCartney!
And although
They may both be dead,
They still live on,
As a part of me!
God bless them,
As they continue to play,
On that great stage above.
Singing the Lord's praises
All you need is love!

Graham Mitchell

SUMMER 1939

'How far away is the sea Mum?
And can we go there soon?
I'm sure it isn't very far I can see it from my room
It looks so blue I can hardly wait!
Here's Dad just coming in the gate
My bucket and spade is here at hand
My sister and I want to play in the sand.
Dad says Let's go to the beach right away,
The sun is hot, it's a lovely day.
We can all go into the sea for a swim
And now our holiday can really begin!
Where are we going so early today?
Down to the Quayside did I hear Dad say ?
The fisherman look so brown
As they fetch in their haul.
The sea is so calm, the ships look so tall.
There's so much to see and so much going on but
Let's go back for breakfast, before it's all gone.
Oh, it's such a nice evening
Can we walk in the sand.
Then on to the Pier, we'll sit watching the band.
I like being out late
And the lights are so pretty,
I wish we could stay
Not return to the city.'

Margaret Pay

IF ONLY, OR SORRY

If only we'd find time to say
I love you in that special way
We know we do and yet it's true
We get wrapped up in what we do.

We all need to hear it, now and then
Not take for granted where or when
Why can't we say it or even try
It seems so simple, so why? Oh why?

Can't we just find the words to say
I love you more in every way
It's not enough to take it for granted
Love is a seed that God has planted.

Love is more than sex in bed
Much, much more than the books you read
So hang on to the love that you possess
Handle it with tenderness.

Remember when you said 'I will'
Remember it, and treasure it still.

Dorothy Sharp Tiffany

MY FAVOURITE THING

My favourite thing is my garden in spring
With daffodils, tulips and more.
Primroses and primulas, yellow and white
And flowers with colours galore.
My favourite thing is my garden in spring
A treasure trove not to be missed
I dig and I hoe, I cut and I mow
With flowers all around me, sun-kissed,
My favourite thing is my garden in spring.
Even daisies that sprout in the lawn
I love them all, the short and the tall
And the birdsong each morning at dawn
My favourite thing is my garden in spring.
With all the hard work it entails
The moss and the weeds, cats uprooting my seeds
Yet my love for it always prevails
I don't care if the housework is long overdue
Or I don't hear the telephone ring.
I'm oblivious to sound that goes on all around
For I do love my garden in spring.

Cathie Bridger

THE SOUP EATERS: EARLY VAN GOGH

A wooden spoon tied soup
To their hunger and sweat
Running from their foreheads,
Shaping their thick eyebrows.

Yet cider then had a colour
Better than sunflowers
Pressed in November
Long after the spring blooms.

Tobacco lost its fragrance
In pockets black with dirt,
With mourning for children
Born to be kings,
                Hiding in charcoal mists.

Marylène Walker

LUCKY ME

Lucky, lucky, lucky me
Life is good and fancy free.
I can run and I can see
Lucky, lucky, lucky me.
I can hear and I can talk,
I can sleep and I can walk.
I can work and I can play,
And I can do this everyday.
Lucky, lucky, lucky me,
I have health and wealth you see,
Wealth in love and food for tea.
Lucky, lucky, lucky me,
I can sew and I can cook,
I can sit and read a book,
I can smell the scent of flowers.
And I can be content for hours.
Lucky, lucky, lucky me.
I can laugh and cry you see,
I can be just plain old me.
Lucky, lucky, lucky me.

Sandy Taylor

FELINE FRIEND
(A Tribute To 'Miss Tibbles')

Blackened fiend, part angel, sharp of tooth and claw
Sit you still upon my lap when it suits your mood
Mew, and tap my newspaper when attention you require
No rest, nor recreation if you prefer to play.

Put down your pen and crossword book, ignore me if you dare,
Throw my bell-ball and tartan mouse for me to chase,
That I may fetch them back again to lay them at your feet,
Three across was 'Generation' by the way, dull fellow.

Pay attention please, that you might comprehend instructions.
'I want to go out' does not sound remotely like 'Feed me!'
Slow human, silly man, so difficult to train.
I, your pet indeed! 'Tis I who own you I believe.

I greet you from the window as the key turns in the latch
Persistent 'Mew' to chastise you. Where have you been all day?
How dare you leave me alone but half the day!
The chicken supper was fine but you aren't forgiven yet.

My turn for angry mewing as I your 'owner' must
Torn fabric, broken vase and knitting wool strewn about.
A month of Mother's Evening Craft is all-a-ruin.
No use wide amber-eyes defiant, best hide if I were you.

Shock and surprise, as unexpectedly you leap upon my shoulder
Pin holes in my jacket, teeth gently nip the ear.
My fur scarf purrs contentedly, carried all about,
Why, oh why my furry pest am I so indulgent?

Gone two days and back again, wet, hungry and bedraggled.
We missed your fickle presence despite all nuisance.
Wicked creature, dear creature all at once in contrast
Little girl much cherished, welcome to our home.

E Morgan

THE BLUEBELL WOOD

The path was inviting, the air warm and still
Passed the swift flowing stream with its old water mill
To the edge of the meadow where the gnarled oak tree stood
Its branches a gateway to the heart of the wood.

My journey continued 'neath cool leafy shade
The sun's dappled rays in the rich forest glade
Small creatures at slumber, a lazy bee's hum
With no one to tell them that day had begun.

Snaking along to a small forest rise
A sight to behold, made me gasp with surprise
Hundreds and thousands in majesty stood
A carpet of blue at the edge of the wood.

Reflection of sky gently soft in the breeze
Nestling resplendent at the foot of the trees
A delicate chime as each blossom expels
To float through my mind merry tinkle of bells.

Bells in profusion on an eiderdown bed
A shimmer of silk, with each small stately head
Graciously nodding as in chorus they stood
Shy ballerinas in the lush bluebell wood.

Through life's busy pathway forever I find
This vision of beauty remains in my mind
A piece of God's Heaven, nature's corner to bring
A joy to my life, and to make my heart sing.

Barbara Davies

THE COLLECTION

Tiger, tiger everywhere
In the cupboard under the stair
On the wall and on the floor
Posters pinned onto the door
On the shelf and on the telly
Some are crawling on their belly
One is sitting on the chair
No two tigers a matching pair
Some are standing others sat
Wipe your feet on the tiger mat
Large and small their sizes vary
Some are cute, cuddly and furry
Some on beautifully painted plates
Others on calendars marking dates
A tiger sits and nods its head
While a mother puts her cub to bed
This large collection is growing weekly
While I take my money and pay up meekly.

Thomas Carey

SHADES OF GREEN

Green is everywhere.
Green is crisp and fresh and inviting,
It is pleasing to the eye
Even sensuous.

Green is everywhere.
Green are the rolling fields of springtime,
And the meadows fresh with dew
And smooth moss on bark.

Green is everywhere.
Green are the trees in the rainforests,
And the proud sweeping willow
Down by the water.

Green is everywhere.
Green are the cool water lily leaves
And the reeds by the mill stream
Where the green ducks swim.

Green is everywhere,
Green is nature, it carpets the earth
The whole year round; then in spring,
New shoots will appear.

Green is everywhere.
Green is food. Grass for the animals,
Fresh vegetables for man
And lush green apples.

Green is everywhere.
Green is vital, for health and constancy,
And home-grown healthy foods.
So then, green is Life.

Phyllis Spooner

THE BEST THINGS ARE NOT FREE

The best things in life are free they say
But that's not always true
The best thing in my life is taken
'cause you know, my friend, it's you.
You give me strength to face the day
Yet we're so very far apart
We cannot be together
Yet you're always in my heart.
We can never be together
Yet I love you so, so much
Your friendship means the world to me
And we're never out of touch.
You make the sun shine brighter
Than it ever has before.
You let me know you love me
When I think you've closed the door,
They say you find love when you least expect
You find gold at the rainbow's end
Well I found more than love or gold
I found my soulmate, my life, my friend.

Margaret Ann Scott

SUNNY DAYS

Listen to the band
Playing near the sand
On a day that is hot and sunny.
The music is loud
Attracting a crowd
Punch and Judy is really quite funny.

Ice-creams and sweets
All kinds of treats
The families are having good fun.
Not a worry or care
Just enjoying the fair
So happy to play in the sun.

The water is cool
In the paddling pool
Why does sand always stick to your toes?
Egg sandwiches too
Taste of sand when you chew
All part of the fun, I suppose.

To the seaside we go
Every John, Jill and Joe
When the sun beams down from the sky.
For sun-kissed days
We give You praise
Father God enthroned on high.

Jean Mackenzie

NIGHT SKY

The moon so pale
The sky so dark blue
Stars shining like diamonds
In a magical fairytale
So romantic, that shooting
Stars appear and disappear
So fast I close my eyes
And listen to the beating
Of my heart thinking of
My loved one.

Olive Irwin

PRICELESS

The best things in life are free
I do believe it's true,
For my favourite things are pure,
And they all come from you.

Memories of holidays,
Lying in the sun,
Laughing in the snow,
Being aeroplanes in the wind.

Smiles, hugs, laughs
All are priceless,
They bring love and blessings
To those that give and those that receive.

All my friends and all my family
Are my favourite things,
They spread a smile on my face,
And wipe away the tears.

Melanie Mockler

GROOM MY HORSE

I must groom my horse and check his feet
So once again me he will be pleased to greet
For after feeding him earlier today
He looks upon the extra time spent with him as play
To generally horse around.

I must groom my horse and check his feet
After calling out the vet again
I cannot understand why he has not got here yet
As I called him out over an hour ago
Over why my horse is coughing many times I need to know
It could be something bad.

I must groom my horse and check his feet
What a day we have had but it was fun so they all said
Dartmoor seems so lonely and yet
Attractive it appears to many though
They will keep going where they do not know
Putting horse and rider at many a risk
Though he never once was startled or tried to kick
Even when we were lost in all the fog
In which we found that child lost
My horse may have caught a chill.

Keith L Powell

A TRUE FRIEND

A gift beyond measure
One I trust and treasure
Is a true friend who cares
Who unselfishly shares
Standing steadfast by me
When life tends to try me
Yet at times when I fail
Gives me no betrayal
Lending needed support
When I'm down and distraught
Who'll unsparingly guide
If my hopes start to slide
Sometimes sad and depressed
Will humour me with jest
Such a friend, in my eyes
Is life's *most* precious prize

Tina Lipman

WHY CAN'T WE ACCEPT AND ADMIRE?

Why can't we accept and admire?
Must we always desire
Better than best . . . ?

System produced
Systematically induced
Wave of, disillusioned, frustration.

No matter what we take in hand . . . it could . . .
It should . . . be the best . . . the very best . . .
In fair contest.

Cultural creation
With elevation, brought forth.
And, everyone proclaims it . . . good.

Ah! . . . But! . . . if only the fools would!
Blind fools! Blind to wonder . . .
Word-assundered . . .

By critical argument . . .
They annihilate integrity . . .
Super-imposing their own superiority . . .

The argument . . . *'If I had made attempt . . .*
I could produce . . . present . . .
Perfection . . .'

I am forced to ask,
Where? This miracle of 'better than?'
And how produced by . . . imperfect 'man'!

Brenda Robson-Eifler

THE SEA

The mighty breakers thunder and roll
Echo and chill to the very soul.

Fierce in its anger the sea tosses and turns,
To be smooth and calm it almost yearns.

Uneasy in its quest to be calm,
It loses all dignity, tranquillity and charm,
Each wave froths and gurgles with great might and mocks -
The silence of all earthly retreats,
On crag-filled rocks it relentlessly beats.

Topsy Pass

MY SEVEN BEST THINGS

Being grabbed by music till your heartstrings twang,
Creamy implosion of a crisp meringue,
Labyrinthine velvet of a baby's ear,
The scent of lilac like Elysian beer,
The awesome lifespan of Sequoia trees,
First summer tasting of your home-grown peas.
Lastly, (and this I'd like in my hereafter),
The raucous, bellyshaking sound of laughter.

These are the joys on which I set great store,
Tomorrow I can give you seven more.

Ruth Parker

SUBMISSIONS INVITED
SOMETHING FOR EVERYONE

POETRY NOW 2000 - Any subject,
any style, any time.

WOMENSWORDS 2000 - Strictly women,
have your say the female way!

STRONGWORDS 2000 - Warning!
Age restriction, must be between 16-24,
opinionated and have strong views.
(Not for the faint-hearted)

All poems no longer than 30 lines.
Always welcome! No fee!
Cash Prizes to be won!

Mark your envelope (eg *Poetry Now) 2000*
Send to:
Forward Press Ltd
Remus House, Coltsfoot Drive,
Woodston,
Peterborough, PE2 9JX

**OVER £10,000 POETRY PRIZES
TO BE WON!**

Judging will take place in October 2000